ENCYCLO

1

HISTORY

Encyclopedia of the Mediterranean
is published jointly by the following publishers
in their respective languages:

Alif-Editions de la Méditerranée, Tunisia
CIDOB-Icaria, Spain
Dar el-Ferjani, Libya
Edisud, France
Editoriale Jaca Book, Italia
Les Editions Toubkal, Morocco
Midsea Books, Malta

DRAGOSLAV SREJOVIĆ

THE ILLYRIANS
AND
THE THRACIANS

Midsea Books
Malta
1998

Published for the first time in 1998
Printed in Malta

General Editor: Louis J. Scerri

Layout:
Mizzi Design & Graphic Services

The Encyclopedia of the Mediterranean
is promoted by an internation association SECUM
- Sciences, Education et Culture en Méditerranée
with offices in Aix-en Provence, Tunisia, Casablanca,
Milan, and Malta.

ISBN: 99909-75-60-4

Further information on this and
other publications may be obtained from
Midsea Books Ltd
Tower Building, Sulphur Lane, Blata l-Bajda HMR 02, Malta
Tel. (+356) 237617, Fax: (+356) 237643
e-mail: kkm@maltanet.net

INDEX

THE ILLYRIANS
AND THE THRACIANS

The Illyrians and the Thracians are the two most enigmatic palaeo-Balkanic peoples. Although they lived from times immemorial in the territories directly associated with the Mediterranean shores and although they were repeatedly involved in the history of the Greeks, the Macedonians, and the Romans, the classical world had a very vague idea of their origin, language, dominions, habits, and customs, for it seems to have been aware of them only when it wanted to make use of them or to defend itself from them. Therefore, all that classical sources say about the Illyrians and Thracians is of questionable reliability. Consequently, the ethnogenesis, culture, history, and customs of these two palaeo-Balkanic peoples are still matters of considerable dispute.

At the time when they enter history, the Thracians

were settled in the eastern and the Illyrians in the south-western parts of the Balkan Peninsula. Thrace was directly linked with the shores of the Black Sea and the Aegean, with Asia Minor, and with the eastern coast of Greece, while Illyria was connected with the Adriatic coastline and the Ionic Sea, i.e. with the western coast of Greece and the eastern coast of Italy (Fig. 1). Since they were also separated by an extensive belt in the central Balkans, settled by peoples and tribes alien to them (the Triballi, the Dardanians, the Peonians, the Macedonians, and so on) no closer contacts were ever established between the Thracians and the Illyrians. In spite of this geographic separation, the destinies of the Thracians and the Illyrians were similar, for they were shaped by the same factors, first by Greek polities and colonies, and then by the Macedonian, Epirian, and Roman states.

Thus the Thracians and the Illyrians never became makers of a joint culture; their states were administered in almost the same way; they were equally fragile and short-lived. And they lost their independence and ultimately their identity under similar circumstances.

The Illyrians and Thracians share, in many respects, the same fate in modern historiography as well. The interest in these two peoples was awakened by the Romantic movement at the end of the eighteenth and beginning of the nineteenth century, primarily as a result of the tendency of the enslaved Balkan peoples

- the Croats, the Serbs, and the Bulgarians - to associate themselves with great and powerful peoples that had lived in their territories in times long past. That Romantic exaltation gave no noteworthy results, but it did create a certain atmosphere of considerable influence on the studies of the Illyrians and the Thracians during the nineteenth century, which were frequently marked by subjectiveness and all sorts of exaggeration. Thus, numerous theories giving the Illyrians and the Thracians an excessively important role in both the classical and the barbarian worlds were advanced (particularly by linguists) in the latter half of the nineteenth century. These theories, supported by archaeologists, remained dominant in the first half of the present century. Thus eminent linguists such as H. Krahe(1955-1964), A. Mayer (1957-1959), and J. Pokorny argued that the Illyrians occupied not only the greater part of the Balkan Peninsula, but also the regions farther north, as far as Germany and Poland. Archaeologists, on the other hand, associated the Illyrians with the makers of some prehistoric cultures, such as the linear pottery culture, the Luzice culture, or the Urnfield culture (C. Schuchardt, G. Kossina, R. Pittioni). Although these cultures never spread to the territories which were considered as Illyrian in classical sources, the 'pan-Illyrian' theories persisted for a long time, as did the 'pan-Thracian' theories, according to which the Thracians dwelt in extensive territories in

9

the central Balkans and in the Lower Danubian region.

A more sober approach was adopted only in the 1960s and 1970s, All the relevant classical sources on the Thracians and the Illyrians came under detailed scrutiny (F. Papazoglu, Ch. Danov, A. Fol, M. Suić, D. Rendić-Miočevic); the available onomastic evidence was also carefully studied (V. Georgijev, R. Katićić); and the relevant numismatic and archaeological finds were also taken into consideration (A. Benac, M. Garašanin, S. Islami, V. Velkov, A. Stipčević, H. Ceka, J. Jurukova). At the same time, other disciplines (physical anthropology, sociology, palaeoethnology, and others) were included in the study of the Illyrians and the Thracians. Thus 'Thracological' and 'Illyrogical' studies have been given a great impetus in the past decades and they have already yielded valuable results concerning the role of the Thracians and the Illyrians in the classical world.

THE ILLYRIANS

Territory, People, Language

Illyria and the Illyrians are first mentioned, only in passing, by Herodotus (*c*.485-425) in his History. He places Illyria round the source of the river Angros (modern Ibar), in a mountainous district in the south-western part of the Balkan Peninsula, and he mentions the Illyrians as the protectors of the fugitive Perdiccas, the future founder of the Macedonian kingdom. He also refers to a prophecy according to which they were a people who would plunder, together with the army of the Enchelei, the Delphic temple and who would perish after that robbery. Thucydides (*c*.460-400) testifies that the Illyrian lands comprised also the south-eastern coastland of the Adriatic. His account of the events which took place in the Peloponessian

Wars, or, more precisely, in 428 BC, shows the Taulantii, an Illyrian people in the immediate vicinity of the Greek colony of Epidamnus (later Dyrrachion, today Durres in Albania), as barbarians, robbers by sea and land, very powerful, although not very ingenious in war tactics, whom both the Macedonians and the Greeks sought to win over as allies. A more detailed account of the Illyrian coastland is given, however, only in Periplos (*c.*330 BC) by an anonymous author called Pseudo-Scylax. He locates the Illyrians, probably basing himself on some earlier sources, south of the Liburnians, along the south-eastern coast of the Adriatic as far as Chaonia and the isle of Corcyra (Corfu). He also lists the tribes dwelling there - the Hierastomnai, the Bouilinoi, the Hylloi, the Nestoi, the Manioi, the Autariatoi, the Enchelei, and the Taulanioi, but only the Enchelei are more precisely located round the Gulf of Kotor. Later sources (Pseudo-Scymnus, Pliny, Strabo, and others) refer specifically to several other Illyrians tribes, including the *Illyrii proprii dicti* (the Illyrians proper), a tribe dwelling probably somewhere in the region of Scodra and Lissus (northern Albania). It was after this tribe that the Greeks named the entire Illyrian people, and the Romans the extensive territory which they occupied in the Balkan Peninsula and which constituted the province of Illyricum in the time of Julius Caesar.

It is not possible to establish the boundaries of Illyria

on the basis of these scant data. Besides, classical authors frequently use the term Illyrians as a general name for various tribes, some of which are definitely non-Illyrian (e g. the Enchslei, the Dardanians). On the other hand, the terms Illyria and Illyrians gradually lost their ethnographic, historical, and political connotations and became mere geographic and administrative designations. This is especially apparent in later sources, dating after the Roman conquest of the Balkan Peninsula. Thus Strabo (65 BC - AD 19) includes the east Alpine tribes in the Illyrians, while Appian (second century) says that the Illyrians occupy all the territories from the Adriatic to the Morava river and from Epirus to the Danube. Appian also reports a myth, known only to him, according to which Illirius, the progenitor of the Illyrians, had as his sons, grandsons, and great-grandsons Enheleus, Autariaus, Dardanus, Medus, Taulantus, Pannonius, Scordiscus, and Triballus, who were the forefathers of the peoples and tribes named after them.

Obviously, Appian's genealogy and his great Illyria, including peoples ethnically and territorially quite distinct from the Illyrians, are artificial constructs, created to meet certain political, fiscal, and administrative considerations after the incorporation of the western regions of the Balkan Peninsula into the Roman Empire. A fairly accurate picture of the Illyrians and their territories can be reconstructed, however, on the basis of a critical analysis of the accounts of the classical historians and geographers cited above.

The term Illyrians, which was originally the name of a single tribe, came to be used for all linguistically and culturally similar tribes dwelling in the territory north of Epirus and west of Macedonia. In the fifth century BC Illyria and the Illyrians extended from the mouth of the River Genusus (modern Shkumbin in central Albania) to the source of the Angros (modern Ibar in northern Montenegro). In the fourth and third centuries BC, the period of the stabilization and prosperity of the Illyrian state, that territory was extended southward to the south of the Aous (modern Vjosa in the southern part of Albania), northward to the mouth of the Narenta (modern Neretva in Herzegovina), and possibly even as far as the Nestos (modern Cetina in Dalmatia). That means that the Illyrians at the time of their greatest prosperity dwelt in the territory bordering on Epirus on the south, on Macedonia on the east, on the lands of the Dardanians and the Pannonians on the north and north-east, and on the territory of the Iapodes, the Delmatae, and the Liburnians of the north-west (Fig. 2). After they had lost their state and independence (in 168 BC), they disintegrated ethnically and territorially. In order to prevent them from reuniting and becoming powerful again, the Romans broke up the large Illyrian tribal communities, giving prominence to small, local clans and stimulating their separatist ambitions. On the other hand, they broke up the territory of the earlier Illyrian State, annexing its southern part to the province of Macedonia, and incorporating its northern region into the province of Dalmatia.

The results of the latest analyses of the remains of the Illyrian language confirm that they inhabited these territories. The Illyrians were not a literate people, and therefore these remains consist only of a few glosses, several hundreds of homonyms and toponyms, as well as a few words preserved in the works of classical writers. The linguistic analysis of these scant remains has nevertheless shown that the Illyrians spoke a distinct Indo-European language, most clearly manifested in the onomastic evidence from the territory associated with the south-eastern coast of the Adriatic from the upper reaches of the Cetina river on the north to the Acroceraunian promontory on the south. This linguistic area, which was undoubtedly Illyrian, is clearly marked off from the adjacent Dalmatian-Pannonian region, i.e. from the territories settled by the Delmatae, the Pannonians, the Liburnians, and the Veneti.

The territory certainly belonging to the Illyrians is not a homogeneous and clearly-defined geographic entity. Approximately at its centre near Shkodra, two regions meet - one associated with the Dinarides and the Adriatic coast, extending NW-SE, and the other, linked with the Pind mountain range and the Adriatic coast, extend-

15

ing N-S. While the Dinarian coastline is rocky, steep, and full of creeks, channels, and clefts, the Pind shore is mostly beachy, with lagoons and extensive fertile plains in the background. These two regions have quite distinct hydrological, climatic, and communication features. The Pind region, i.e. southern Illyria, has rivers with abundant water flowing in the E-W direction, along whose transverse valleys the Mediterranean climate and vegetation penetrated far into the hinterland. It is a region with dense vegetation and soil suitable for farming, but with two great geographical setbacks: the shore is rocky and unsuitable for maritime and overland communication, and the entire region is, in relation to the Balkan Peninsula as a whole, rather peripheral and lies outside the main longitudinal traffic lines. The northwestern part of Illyria, linked with the Dinarides, has a coastline suitable for maritime traffic, but it has no fertile land in the hinterland and no major river flowing into the Adriatic Sea. Apart from the Beli Drim, all the rivers with sources in north Illyria flow into the Sava and the Danube, i.e. they belong to the Black Sea basin. As a result, the influence of the Mediterranean climate is very limited, and since the land is almost entirely mountainous and exposed to the harsh continental climate, is only suitable for the semi-nomadic type of livestock raising.

Such geographic and climatic conditions of Illyria exercised a great influence on the life of its inhabitants. Because of the lack of communications in their

16

territory, the Illyrians never achieved complete cultural and political unity. Even in the central Illyrian region the inhabitants were segregated into separate tribes as late as the end of the fifth century BC, and it was only occasionally that they formed minor tribal alliances. This situation remained unaltered in the peripheral districts until the time of the Roman conquests. The authority of the chieftain was always confined to the territory of the tribe. The discord among the Illyrians, frequently referred to in classical sources, was a result of profound differences in the economy and the general culture of the individual tribes as well as of the dissimilarities of their customs and religious concepts. These differences were aggravated by their unequal contacts with the neighbouring peoples. The tribes in southern Illyria, which lived in the hinterland of Greek colonies and which were directly exposed to the influence of Greek culture, became culturally distinct at a comparatively early date from the tribes settled in northern Illyria, which continued to adhere to prehistoric forms of life for a long period of time. The integration processes in Illyria were constantly impeded by a number of internal and external factors. It is because of this that, even in the period of the greatest ascendancy of the Illyrian State, Illyrian tribes did not coalesce into an integrated ethnic entity, nor did they develop a culture of their own.

The formation of the Illyrian people was a long and complex process which took place in a period unknown to history. The earliest contacts between the Illyrians and the Mediterranean civilization were reflected partly in Greek myths, but what had happened before that in their territory can be surmised only on the basis of archaeological finds. Although these finds are numerous, they are far from informative enough for a reliable reconstruction of the ethnogenesis of the Illyrians.

Since the 1960s, when the theory according to which the Illyrians came from Central Europe in the north was finally abandoned, scholarly attention has been focused on the archaeological finds indicating the presence of the Indo-Europeans in the future Illyrian territories. The majority of Yugoslav and Albanian archaeologists are now inclined to associate burial under mounds, documented in Albania and Montenegro in the Eneolithic and the Early Bronze Age (third early - second millennium BC) with the earliest presence of the Indo-Europeans in these regions. Since the local culture developed continuously from that time on, it has been assumed that it provides evidence of the ethnogenesis of the Illyrians. The first stage, termed pre-Illyrian, is thought to be characterized by the merging of the culture of the autochthonous population with the culture of the Indo-European immigrants during the Neolithic and the Early Bronze Age. The culture developed in the subsequent phase, in the fully developed Bronze Age (second millennium BC), is associated with the proto-Illyrians, and the culture of the Early Iron Age (late second-early first millennium BC) is associated with the Ur-Illyrians, while the culture of the period between the eighth and fifth centuries BC was already developed by the Illyrians.

This attractive theory is, however, difficult to substantiate by archaeological finds. During the third millennium BC there arrived, indeed, members of a mobile population coming from the north and the north-east who buried their chiefs under large mounds sometimes with costly weapons (Fig 3a). It is, however, risky to associate these individual mounds with any major ethnic group which assimilated the native population and affected the Indo-Europization of this part of the Balkan Peninsula. On the other hand, no specific culture developed in the classical Illyrian territory in the Bronze Age: the Maliq III culture became established in southern Albania, the Dinara-Cetina culture emerged in northern Albania and in Montenegro, and various local cultures sprang up in the more distant hinterland. It is significant, however, that from about 1600 BC bronze weapons (curved knives, swords) began to appear in the territory of future Illyria, indicating trade links with the Aegean world, and, particularly, with Mycenean culture (Fig. 3b). The bronze axes of an unusual shape (the Shkodra type axes), common on several sites in Albania and Montenegro (Fig. 3c), are probably also associated with the Mediterranean world. The character of these links is not clear. The relations between the eastern Mediterranean world and the populations settled on the south-eastern coast of the Adriatic in this period are probably partly reflected in some Greek myths, particularly the story of Kadmos, in which Illyria and the Illyrians are accorded a conspicuous place.

There are a number of traditions narrating what brought Kadmos, the founder of Beotian Thebes, and his wife Harmonia to the south-eastern shores of the Adriatic, and what happened to them afterwards. The story has it that Kadmos, when he grew very old, was compelled to leave Thebes and to go, together with his wife, to the Enshelei, the people of the eels, who lived north of Epirus, or between the Boka Kotorska bay and Durris. It had been prophesied to the Enchelei that they would defeat their neighbours the Illyrians, the people of the serpents, if they chose a newcomer for their leader. They did so and chose Kadmos, who overcame the Illyrians and became the lord of their country. In the new kingdom Harmonia bore him a son, Illyrius, after whom the entire country was named. Soon afterwards Kadmos led an expedition of the united Enchelei and Illyrians against Greece, and this barbarian force was victorious until it attempted to plunder Delphi. Then their army was routed, and Xadmos and Harmonia returned to the shores of the Adriatic, where they were metamorphosed into serpents.

It is difficult to say whether, and to what extent, the myth of Kadmos's stay among the Enchelei is a reflection of actual events. It is almost certain that the Enchelei had settled in southern Illyria in a very early period and that the Illyrians, who came to live in their vicinity, gradually mixed with them and formed a united Illyrian kingdom. The myth describes Kadmos as a great wanderer who had travelled from Sidon to the south-eastern shores of the Adriatic, a route which may have been a reminiscence of the actual movements of peoples and merchandise between these two regions during the Bronze Age.

Our knowledge of the period between 1200 and 700 BC in the Illyrian territories is based only on scant archaeological finds. Links with the Mediterranean world were severed in this period, but contacts with the populations settled in the island regions of the Balkan Peninsula became stronger, and there began to appear bronze swords of Central European origin. The appearance of settlements located on elevated places difficult of access indicate major upheavals. Some of these settlements, e.g. Gajtan near Shkodra, were fortified by walls built of limestone blocks and up to 3.5 metres thick (Fig. 4a). These walls enclosed remains of modestly-furnished dwellings made of timber and mud. It would seem that these settlements were occupied only occasionally as places of refuge.

It was only towards the end of the eighth century BC that integration processes leading to the emergence of several major ethnocultural entities made themselves felt in all Illyrian territories. They became clear only in the sixth-fifth centuries BC. During this period the earliest Greek colonies were also established on the south-eastern shores of the Adriatic Epidamnos (Dyrrachium, modern Durres), founded by Corcyra and Corinth c.627 BC, and Apollonia, founded by Corinth c.588 BC - which exercised a strong influence on the Illyrian tribes in their hinterland and introduced the Illyrians to history. A culture of the Kuc-Zi type emerged in the territory south of the Shkumbin river, while a well-integrated culture developed farther north. Several regional variants can be distinguished within the latter culture: the Mat culture (central Albania), the Kukes-Drilon culture (north-eastern Albania and Metohija), the Lisje Polje culture (north Montenegro), and the Glasinac culture (south-eastern Bosnia). Mounds with over a hundred burials have been discovered in the region of the Kuc-Zi culture, which testifies to the existence of large tribal communities. The jewellery from these graves is associated mainly with Macedonian and Greek workshops. The archaeological finds from the mounds in the northern districts are quite different. The Mat culture graves contained various personal adornments, and the burials belonging to the Kukes-Drilon and Glasinac cultures were accompanied by weapons and war gear. From as early as the seventh century BC, the number of warrior burials steadily increased in the entire north Illyrian territory, the most remarkable being the graves of tribal chiefs, which contained costly war equipment, bronze vessels, and amber jewellery. It would seem that integrative processes noticeable in the culture of the seventh-fifth centuries were initiated in the region with the earliest rich warrior burials, i.e. in the region of the Glasinac culture. The weapons and adornments of the representatives of this culture were adopted by the neighbouring communities, i.e. by the representatives of the Lisje Polje, the Mat, and the Kukes-Drilon cultures (Fig. 5). These cultures were probably developed by individual tribes known from later historical sources - the Glasinac culture may be associated with the Autariatae, the Lisje Polje culture with the Ardiaei, the Mat culture with the Taulantiii, the Kukes-Drilon culture with the Illyrians proper, and the Kuc-Zi culture, which differs greatly from the others, with the Enchelei or Briganes, i.e. a separate people only later assimilated by the Illyrians.

During the fifth century, in the period immediately preceding the foundation of the first Illyrian kingdom, the culture from the Greek colonies on the Adriatic coast began to penetrate increasingly into the hinterland, and this led to the gradual acculturization of the earlier regional cultures. Specific traits of the local cultures were ousted out by the levelling influence of the dominant alien forms, and this led to the emergence of an eclectic and very impoverished culture in which it is difficult to distinguish what is Illyrian and what is Greek, Macedonian, Epirian, or Italic. The integrating process is noticeable only in the appearance of a new type of settlements and in the considerably improved communication lines, as evidenced by the increased flow of goods and money. On the other hand, it is apparent that the centre of integration had shifted from the north to the south, where a number of new settlements sprang up at the end of the fifth century and in the fourth century BC. In addition to Greek colonies, there developed native 'towns', such as Byllis and Pelion, which were in fact centres of economic activities surrounded by villages. These 'towns' were well defended and located at the centre of minor geographic entities, possibly the territories of individual tribes, suitable for farming, livestock breeding, or mining. It was as a result of the unification of the economic and political interests of such entities that the first Illyrian kingdoms emerged.

The common economic interest of the Illyrian tribes was the plundering of their rich neighbours on the mainland and in the sea, and their political interest was the defence from the external enemy, usually the same plundered neighbours, i.e. the inhabitants of Macedonia, Epirus, and Greek colonies. The first Illyrian kings were probably only tribal chieftains who had succeeded in placing themselves at the head of a tribal league, sufficiently strong to defend its own and occupy other people's territories.

If we neglect the legendary Illyrian kings - Kadmos and Galauros - or Grabos and Sirrhas, known by name only - the first king of Illyria referred to in historical sources is Barylis. It is known that he reigned some time between 393 and 359/8 BC and that he had an army which seriously threatened Macedonia and compelled its kings to pay tribute to the Illyrians. It was in an encounter with the Illyrian forces that Perdiccas III and 4,000 Macedonian soldiers perished in 360 BC. Macedonia was liberated from the Illyrians only by the energetic Philip II. In a major battle waged in 359 BC, he routed Bardylis and his army, which consisted of 10,000 infantrymen and 500 horsemen. The Illyrians lost 7,000 men and, probably, a part of their territories. A few years later Grabos, the king of Illyria, tried, with the help of the Thracians and the Paeones, to stem the rigid rise of the Macedonian state.

From that time until *c.*270 BC the Illyrians and their kingdoms are mentioned only sporadically in the history of Macedonia and Epirus. In 344 BC, at the time of King Pleuratos, Philip II devastated Illyria again; King Kleitos tried to rid himself of the Macedonian domination in 335 BC, but he was utterly beaten and had to cede his country to the Macedonians and seek shelter from Glaukias, the king of the Taulantii. Around 295 BC the king of the Illyrians was Bardulis I, probably the grandson of Bardulis I, who had given his daughter in marriage to Pyrrhus, the king of Epiirus and allowed him to annex the southern Illyrian territories, including Apollonia. From about 280 BC the king of Ilyria was Monounions whose name appears on the coins of Epidamnus, and all we know about his successor Mytilos is that he minted his own money and that he waged war against Pyrrhus's son Alexander, *c.*270 BC. It is not known which territories were included into the domains of these kings. It is only certain that during the fourth century the Illyrian forces were concentrated in the continental regions of Illyria and that the centre of the Illyrian state began to gravitate towards the coastal regions during the third century.

Around the middle of the third century the conditions on the borders between Macedonia and Epirus were peaceful, and the Illyrians took advantage of that lull to furnish themselves with light and fast boats (*lemboi*), which became the terror of the inhabitants of the Adriatic and Ionic coastlands. A few decades later a new Illyrian state, well-organized, powerful both on land and sea, emerged in the territory extending from Epirus in the south to Dardania in the north and from Macedonia in the east to Liburnia in the west. When Agron, the king of Illyria, routed the united army of the Aetolian and Achaian league - the greatest powers of Greece - the entire Mediterranean world shook with dread of the new barbarian danger looming in the north.

In the new Illyrian state, which consisted of towns and tribal communities of varying size, the power of the king was hereditary and supra-tribal. Important affairs were entrusted to the members of the royal house or to the 'king's friends', who included some Greeks as well. The king had at his disposal vast riches acquired by the taxation of his subjects. Agron had immense land and maritime forces and his subjects developed piracy into a veritable economic activity: they intercepted Greek and Italian ships, plundered their cargo and pillaged fields and towns on alien shores. The possibility of rapid and easy acquisition of a rich booty led to the neglect of the earlier economic activities - livestock raising, farming and the cultivation of vine and olive. These plundering expedition led, however, to the decline of the Illyrian state.

After Agron's death, his widow Teuta assumed the rule and, having mustered a considerable fleet and accompanying troops, she sent them out to sea, instructing them to treat all other countries as enemies and to plunder them mercilessly. The Illyrians first seized the richest Epirian town, Phoinike. After that they robbed and murdered many Italian merchants and threatened Issa, the most important Greek colony on the Dalmatian islands, as well as Corcyra and Epidamnus. The Romans sent their fleet and troops to succour these towns. They overcame the Illyrian forces in a short time and compelled Teuta to pay tribute to the Roman state and to cede to it most of her territories.

The ensuing developments led to the consolidation of the Roman state in the Balkan Peninsula and to the collapse of the Illyrian state. Agron's son Pinnes and brother Scerdilaidas organized other plundering expeditions, but the Romans crushed them in the so-called Second Illyrian War (219 BC). After this defeat Scerdilaidas and his son Pleuratos sided with the Romans in their conflict with Philip V of Macedonia. At the beginning of the second century BC, the Roman army invaded Apollonia and Dyrrachium, occupying all the eastern Illyrian territories, including the ancient Illyrian town of Pelion, and established a base for the war against Macedonia. Pleuratos's son, Genthios, sought, about 118 BC, to unite the Illyrians, the Macedonians and the Dardanians in a defensive alliance against the Romans. He managed to organize a large fleet consisting of 270 ships and to muster 15,000 troops, but the Romans brought to the Illyrian shores twice as many soldiers commanded by Lucius Anicius, who annihilated the Illyrian forces gathered in Schodra in a matter of days. Genthios himself was taken captive together with his entire family, and Anicius celebrated a triumph in Rome, in which the entire wealth captured in Illyria was displayed: 27 pounds of gold, 16 pounds of silver, and a vast quantity of money. In 167 BC Anicius dictated the conditions of peace to the Illyrian chieftains summoned to Schodra: Illyria was divided into three regions. The Illyrians towns and tribes that had sided with the Romans during the war were exempt from all taxes, and the taxes of the other Illyrians were reduced to a half of what they had had to pay to their king.

This marked the end of the Illyrian state. In the subsequent decades some Illyrian towns and tribes managed to preserve a certain degree of independence, and some dynasty, such as King Ballaios, who probably kept his court in Rhizon, even minted their own money during their brief reign. These were, however, a greater semblance of freedom meant gradually to accustom the Illyrians to the final enslavement, which was to take place in the time of Caesar and Octavian.

The Illyrians spent the two-and-a-half centuries of their independence mainly in waging wars against the

Macedonians, the Greeks, the Epirians, and the Romans. The periods of peace were too short for the development of a specifically Illyrian culture. Archaeological evidence shows that the Illyrians supplied most of their needs with foreign imports even in the period of their independence. Their towns betray traces of the influence of Epirian, Macedonian, or Greek building and architecture, and the same applies to their handicrafts. The entire Illyrian material culture in the fourth-second centuries BC was strongly influenced by Hellenistic and Celtic or La Tène culture. This is most apparent in the grave goods discovered in Illyrian cemeteries. The grave of an Illyrian chieftain from the middle of the fourth century BC discovered in Belsh (southern Albania) contained war gear modelled on the equipment of Greek *hoplitoi*, as well as bronze and earthenware vessels imported from the adjacent Greek colonies. The graves in Rhizon and Buthos dating from the fourth and third centuries BC yielded pottery from south Italian workshops, as well as Hellenistic jewellery, while third- and second-century graves discovered at Gostilj (Herzegovina) and Momišići (Montenegro) contained, in addition to Hellenistic ware, jewellery typical of the Celtic culture (Fig. 6).

In the third and fourth centuries Illyrian towns were in full prosperity. In addition to some earlier urban centres, new towns sprang up, both in the southern parts of the country (Dimale, Antipatrea, Albanopolis) and in the northern and north-western regions (Lissus, Scodra, Olcinium, Buthoe, Rhizon). These new towns usually consisted of a fortified acropolis and a settlement below it, which was frequently walled in, too. The defence walls were regularly built of large polygonal blocks, and the gates were sometimes flanked by towers (Fig. 4b). Byllis, one of the largest towns in Illyria, had six such gates and its walls, more than 2,000 metres long, enclosed an area of 30 hectares (Fig. 4c). Little is known of the internal structure of these towns apart from the fact that the area with dwellings was separated from the district with workshops in at least some of them. Byllis had a large agora, a stadium, a cistern, and a theatre seating about 7,000 spectators.

Other aspects of the Illyrian culture, such as art and religion, are documented by few archaeological finds only. Judging by these, Illyrian art never exceeded the level of mere technical competence nor developed a style of its own. Among the toreutic and earthenware products of the seventh and sixth centuries BC, there are a few original works (e.g. weapons and jewellery of the Glasinac culture of some pottery of the Kukes-Drilon culture). On the whole, however, this production is characterized by stereotyped forms, monotonous geometric ornaments, and imitation of Greek and Italian models. The process of urbanization during the fifth-third centuries BC interrupted the further development of traditional crafts. Town populations used mainly products imported from the Greek colonies on the Adriatic coast or from Italy and Attica, while local masters catered for the poorest classes only.

Just as the Illyrians did not achieve an art style of their own, so they never succeeded in forming a coherent spiritual world or a Pantheon. Historical sources provide no evidence of the religion of any Illyrian tribe, and the relevant archaeological finds are not only scant, but also chiefly associated with magic rites and superstitions found in other palaeo-Balkanic peoples, too.

The bronze chariot with water fowls (Fig. 7a) or the discoid pendants from Glasinac (sixth century BC) are frequently cited as evidence of the worship the Sun among the northern Illyrian tribes, while etymological speculations about the name Illyria (snake) and the finds of bracelets ending in snake heads have given rise to the theory that this reptile was accorded the greatest respect in the southern Illyrian lands. An amber pendant showing a horseman, found in Lisje Polje and dating from the fifth century BC (Fig. 7b), deserves greater attention since Medaurus, the patron of Rhizon mentioned in a Roman inscription from Lambaesis (second century BC), is also represented as a horseman. The worship of a horse-mounted protective deity among the Illyrians is also attested by several late third-century belt buckles found at Selce (Albania) and Gostilj (Montenegro), which show a horseman, with a serpent behind him, who destroys enemies (Fig. 7c). A buckle from Gostilj and a ring from Momišići show, besides, a seated female figure with a bird in her hand, perhaps the Illyrians supreme deity, similar to Greek Aphrodite or Artemis (Fig. 7d).

Little is known about Illyrian shrines. It is surmised that isolated mounds frequently found near fortified settlements, which contain layers of burnt material with a large quantity of fragmented vessels, were cult places. It is a moot point whether certain people among the Illyrians performed priestly duties. Human sacrifice seems to have been practised, for Arianus (*c.* 95-175) reports that the defenders of the Illyrian town Pelion sacrificed three boys, three little girls, and three black rams. Very old totemistic concepts can be recognized in the names of some tribes (the Enchelei = the people of the eels; the Taulantii = the people of the swallows) or towns (Ulcinium, from *uclos* = wolf). It is possible that weapons were also worshipped (hololatry): separately buried swords or spears were found in the centre of several tribal capitals, and a belt buckle from Gostilj shows a spear flanked by gryphons.

The Illyrians believed in an afterlife. Weapons, jewellery, and various vessels found in their graves show that they were confident that they would wage wars and participate in merry feasts after death. Large mounds with complicated grave structures found in cemeteries dating from the seventh-fifth centuries BC indicate that in some cases the cult of the dead developed into hero worship. The late third-century rock tombs at Selca (Albania), in which presumably kings or tribal chiefs were buried, were probably associated with that cult. Their façades, decorated with Ionic columns and ox heads, follow Hellenistic models. The process of Romanization, which set in after the collapse of the Illyrian state, led to the gradual intermingling of traditional Illyrian heroes, deities and local customs with those of the Romans.

The Illyrians within the Roman Empire

After Rome's victory over Genthios, the Illyrian countries fell into complete oblivion. For an entire century the subdued Illyrians are not referred to in historical sources, and there is no archaeological evidence enabling us to say anything definite about their fate. It is only during the Roman civil wars, particularly at the time of the conflict between Caesar and Pompey that the Illyrian coastland re-emerges into the full light of history. By that time the population of former Illyrian towns had substantially changed. Roman names begin to appear in the maritime zone, and a 'community of Roman citizens' is mentioned in Lissus. From 44 BC Roman *denarii* gradually ousted out 'Illyrian drachmae', and Italian amphorae with wine and costly Roman ware (*terra siglata*) began to reach major urban centres. After the battle of Actium (31 BC) the former 'free towns' became Roman colonies - such as Dyrrhacium and Byllis - and Scodra, Lissus, Buthoe, and Rhizon on are referred to as 'towns of Roman citizens'. Latin was introduced in all the territories north of the river Mat, and Greek remained in use only in the more southern Illyrian lands.

Archaeological investigations have shown that there was a revival and even territorial expansion of the Illyrian coastal towns already in the early first century BC. Their cemeteries (e.g. in Buthoe) document only Roman forms of burial, and grave monuments record mostly foreign names from Italy, Greece, Asia Minor, or Syria. Buildings with luxurious floor mosaics dating from the first and second centuries and cemeteries laid out in imitation of the graveyards in major urban centres such as Salona or Aquileia have been discovered in Buthoe and Rhizon. In Dyrrhacium a large amphitheatre seating more than 15,000 spectators, spacious baths, and public edifices with floor mosaics were built during the second century.

Archaeological finds from the first three centuries AD found in the hinterland, where the natives were concentrated round small agricultural holdings or mines, give us a much more interesting picture. During the first century the inhabitants of these regions continued to bury their dead in the traditional way and to accompany them with hand-made earthenware vessels. The process of

Romanization made itself felt only from the second century onward, and particularly during the reigns of Hadrian and Antoninus Pius, when several settlements grew into towns, which were granted the rights of a municipium. At the end of the second century, at the time of the crisis which affected the Illyrian maritime towns, the Illyrian population in the hinterland made its last independent appearance - this time in the cultural sphere. This Illyrian revival is most fully illustrated by the reliefs on third-century grave monuments, the style of which closely resembles that of some prehistoric forms. The figures on these reliefs are modelled without any feeling for the third dimension and for spatial arrangement. Strange proportions and constant wavering between realistic details and decorative elements impart a special charm to these monuments and represent an important aspect of the still vital native artistic tradition (Figs. 8 a-d).

This revival of traditional forms lasted until the incursions of barbarian peoples into the Balkan Peninsula during the fourth century. This threat led to the homogenization of the population in all Roman provinces. The Illyrians and the other Balkan peoples became the main factor in the Roman army during the third and fourth centuries and the most important guardians of the Roman civilization. Diocletian's administrative reforms at the end of the third century and the rapid spreading of Christianity during the fourth century obliterated all the ethnic and cultural differences in Illyricum that had existed before. The former Illyrian territories became parts of three provinces - Epirus Nova, Praevalis, and Dalmatia - by the early years of the fourth century at the latest. After the definitive disintegration of the Roman Empire in 395, Dalmatia became a part of the Western Roman Empire, and Praevalis and Epirus Nova were included into the Eastern Empire.

The ethnicity of the populations of such administratively-fragmented territories became totally unimportant: they had all become loyal subjects of the Roman state and adherents of Christianity, and all their energy was concentrated on the defence from the barbarians. Whatever they did in the period between the fourth and sixth century was motivated either by the fear of the barbarians or by the belief in the new god. Former minor settlements like Scampis (modern Elbasan in Albania) became large military camps, and churches and baptisteries, frequently with luxurious floor mosaics (the basilicas in Saranda, Arapaj, Byllis, Antigoneia, and Lin) were built in almost all towns. None of these buildings, however, bears any specific Illyrian traits. Archaeological and epigraphic evidence shows that the Illyrians disappeared completely as an ethnic entity in the course of the fourth century. The latest reference to the Illyrians in the Life of Dematrius, the martyr from Thessaloniki, compiled in the early sixth century, has a merely administrative and not ethnic connotation.

During their nearly thousand-year-long history the Illyrians left deep traces in the developments in the Mediterranean. The role they played in the Macedonian-Roman wars was of a decisive political importance, and their territory was a stage of crucial developments at the time of the Roman civil wars. Their significance in the economic and cultural history of the classical world is still not sufficiently known. The myth of Xadmos is certainly not pure fiction, but a memory of the economic and cultural links between the most eastern shores of the Mediterranean, Greece, and the Adriatic, in which the Illyrians certainly played a very important role.

THE THRACIANS

Thrace and the Thracians in Myth and Reality

'Before Scythia, towards the sea, is Thrace ... No one can say what lies north of that country and who dwells there... The Thracians are, after the Indians, the most numerous people in the world... They have many appellations, according to their several provinces, and their customs are almost identical ....'

Herodotus's account of Thrace and the Thracians is based less on the knowledge of Greek geographers and ethnographers than on the Greek traditions, preserved in myths and poetry, that north of the shores of the Aegean lie vast territories inhabited by the Thracians. According to these beliefs, the Thracian territories were a separate continent comprising a quarter of the world. Therefore Thrace, the eponymic heroine of the

Thracian lands, was considered the sister of Europa and half-sister of Asia and Libya. Even some later classical sources described all the parts of the Balkan Peninsula, from the Adriatic to the Black Sea, as Thracian territories, and, consequently, all the peoples that dwelt in them were considered as Thracians. Thus the Thracians were said to include not only the peoples living in their immediate neighbourhood - the Getae, the Mysi, the Triballi, and the Paeones - but also groups dwelling on the opposite side of the Balkan Peninsula, several thousand kilometres away from them - e.g. the Istri and the Daorsae. On the other hand, myths and Homeric lays frequently associate Thracian heroes and kings with specific regions in Macedonia, central Greece, or Asia Minor. This fact was used later as proof that the Thracians did actually inhabit all these territories.

This Great Thrace existed, however, only in myths and legends. The southern and eastern boundaries of Thrace were known to be Greeks from early times, but its northern, and, particularly, western, frontiers remained vague for a long time. The Homeric epics (eighth century BC) already define the southern boundary of Thrace as lying on the northern shores of the Aegean and the Propontis, while its eastern frontier became known to the Greeks in the course of the seventh century BC, when they founded their colonies on the western shores of Pontus and found the Thracians already settled there.

The Greeks used the long chain of their colonies, extending from the mouth of the Strymon (modern Struma) to Bosphorus and from Bosphorus to the mouth of the Danube, to exploit not only the resources of the Thracian land (grain, meat, timber, metals) but also to gather valuable information on the geographic features of the central parts of the Balkan Peninsula and on the peoples settled there. Hecatasus (*c*.500 BC) tried to give a general account of Thrace of the basis of this information, and he thought that it included all the lands from the northern shores of the Aegean to the Danube and from the western shores of the Pontian Sea to the Axios river (modern Vardar). He did point, however, that Mount Haimos (modern Balkan) marked the northern boundary of Thrace proper. Subsequent geographers and historians made substantial corrections of the western boundary of Thrace only. First it was transferred from the Axios to the Strymon, and later to the Nestos (modern Mesta). That means that Thrace had natural boundaries to the north (Haimos) and the west (the Struma or Mesta, i.e. mountains Rila and Pirin - Fig. 1).

Archaeological and linguistic researches have also shown that these were the real boundaries of Thrace. Throughout prehistory, the culture in the basin of the Hebros river (modern Marica), which is the core region of Thrace, was clearly distinct from the cultures north of Haimos and west of the Rhodopes. On the other hand, the peoples living in the regions north and west of these mountain ranges (the Getae, the Mysi, the Triballi, the Peonians, and the Macedonians) spoke languages different from that of the Thracians. This does not mean, however, that the Thracians remained within these boundaries throughout their long history. Some of their tribes inhabited, for a longer or shorter period, territories north of Haimos or west of the Mesta and the Struma, but these tribes never took part in any major historic undertaking, and they were always of marginal importance.

Thrace is a large basin enclosed on the north, west, and south by extensive mountain ranges, while its south-eastern and eastern parts are open to the shores of the Aegean, the Propontis, and the Pontus. Although it represents an almost ideal geographic entity, Thrace was a land full of contrasts. Its eastern parts were influenced by the steppe climate, its southern and central regions had Mediterranean climatic conditions, and its western and northern territories belonged to the zone of harsh continental climate. Homer sings of the snowy peaks of Thracian mountains, but he also praises the fertile Thracian country, 'mother of sleep' and 'the homeland of the swiftest horses'. In mythology, Thrace is the homeland not only of the north wind Boreas, but also of Zephyr, the god of the western wind which brings spring showers and heralds warm weather. It is a country rich in mineral resources, very fertile for the most part, suitable for livestock-raising, farming, the growing of vines, olives and fruit, as well as for hunting and fishing. It was precisely because of these diverse riches that the Greeks from Miletus, Clasmen, Athens, Megara, Corinth, Chios, Paros, and Samos colonized, in the course of the seventh-sixth centuries BC, the entire Thracian coast land and acquired first-hand knowledge of the native population and its manners and customs.

The first contacts between the Greeks and the inhabitants of Thrace were probably established much earlier, during the latter half of the second millennium BC, but the only evidence of them is to be found in Greek myths or in *The Iliad* and *The Odyssey*. The Greek heroes who came to Thrace were usually not welcomed. The Thracian king Diomedes fed his mares on human flesh and had all the foreigners who came to his country thrown before them. Lycurgus, king of the Thracian Edones, frightened the god Dionysos himself when he first set foot on Thracian ground, and Kings Tereus and Phineus aroused the hatred of both people and gods because of their cruelty, ferocity, and treachery.

On the other hand, myths and legends stress the great valour, exceptional musical talent and knowledge of divine mysteries of the Thracians. In the Trojan war the Thracians are the allies of the Trojans and bitter enemies of the Greeks, but their king Rhesus, who comes to the walls of Troy furnished with golden arms and with horses whiter than snow, is a noble warrior who is transformed into a demigod after his death. Thrace is a country of renowned musicians, poets, seers and priests: Orpheus, Tamyris, Linus, and Eumolpus. Orpheus is not only the most famous musician and poet, but also the earliest Thracian king who united the Thracians and the Macedonians and reformed the Thracian religion. The enigmatic, controversial person, associated with the darkness of the underworld and the radiance of the heaven, a priest of both Dionysos and Apollo, was largely responsible for the later image of Thrace as a country inhabited by a people of strange customs and manners, completely different from the Greeks.

The Greeks were the first to acquire first-hand knowledge, not based on myth and legend but on actual observation, of the inhabitants of south-eastern Thrace. In the Homeric epics, which reflect the conditions in the Thracian lands between the thirteenth and the eighth centuries BC, the Thracians, allies of the Trojans, are settled in the region between the Hebros and the sea, the Sinti live on the island of Lemnos, while the northern shores of the Aegean, between the mouth of the Nestos and the Hebros, are inhabited by the Kikones. It was only at the time of the colonization of the northern shores of the Aegean and the western coast land of the Pontian Sea that the Greeks learned something about the Thracian tribes in the Balkan hinterland Hecataeus, Herodotus, and some later classical authorities mention a number of Thracian tribes not only in the eastern part of the Balkan Peninsula, but also on the Aegean isles of Samothrace, Thasos, and Imbros, (Lesbos), in the Propontis, and in Asia Minor. Because of that, Greek sources frequently refer to a large part of the Aegean as the Mare Thracium. The Hebros valley, the core of Thrace, was the most densely inhabited. The central part was settled by the Odrysai; east of them, towards the Black Sea, lived the Astai and Thynoi; the southern regions, towards the Dardanelles, were inhabited by the Apsinthioi and Dolonkoi, and the western parts belonged to the Bessi. The Rhodopes and the adjacent districts were settled by the Satrai, and the territories south-west of them, towards the Aegean, were inhabited by the Bistones. The territories to the north-east, towards the Getae and the Danube, were inhabited by the Koilaletai, Nipsaoioi, and Krobyzoi (Fig. 9).

The major Thracian tribes (e.g. the Odrysae, Bessoi, Krobyzoi) included a number of small clans; in other words, they were tribal alliances headed by a king who had originally performed both secular and sacred duties. The people lived in villages, and the tribal aristocracy dwelt in strongholds which were built in southern Thrace already in the course of the ninth-eighth centuries BC and in the northern regions during the seventh-sixth centuries BC. The inhabitants in the continental parts were dependent mainly on hunting and livestock-breeding, and, to a considerably lesser degree, on farming; in the maritime regions and on the islands they mostly lived off piracy and plunder. The basic social unit was a polygamous family. Herodotus records that the Thracians allow their girls to give themselves freely to men, but that they guard their wives jealously and that they buy them at great cost, although they sell their children abroad. Leisure is something that they value most, and farming is greatly abhorred. To live off war and plunder is considered to be the most honourable. People engaged in manual crafts (and even their children) are regarded as socially inferior, and tattooing is a sign of nobility (Fig. 10a).

Herodotus also describes the Thracian customs accompanying birth and death. Members of the Trausoi tribe wail at the birth of a child because of the troubles that await him, and they bury their dead with great cheer, mentioning the woes that they will avoid. The wealthy Thracians were exposed and mourned for three days after their death. After that they were either cremated or interred, and a mound was heaped above their grave and various contests were organized on that site. The wife dearest to the deceased was killed by her next of kin and buried in her husband's grave.

Thucydides mentions the proclivity of the Thracians to hoard riches and accept bribes, and he says that they can behave like the most bloodthirsty barbarian tribes if they can do it with impurity. It is known that they wore long multicoloured and garish hempen shirts and cloaks, caps made of fox fur, and footwear made of deer skin (Fig. 10b). They were variously armed: some tribes had javelins, short swords and small wickerwork shields, while some others wielded long swords. The kings wore gold and silver armour, and archaeological finds show that the Thracian aristocracy had jewellery and drinking vessels made of precious metals. The deposits of gold and silver in southern Thrace, in Samothrace, and in Thasos were not exploited by the natives only. The Persians, the Athenians, and the Macedonians were also interested in them.

The language of the Thracians, known only by personal and tribal names, geographical terms, and a few glosses, is one of the Indo-European languages which linguistic science has not been able to define more precisely yet. In the course of time that language absorbed a number of words from the languages of the neighbouring peoples, primarily the Greeks and the Macedonians. Some Thracian kings spoke excellent Greek, and some of them had Greek or Macedonian wives. The Thracians, however, did not have a script of their own; classical writers record that they could count up to four only and that they considered the use of an alphabet despicable. The extant Thracian texts show, however, that they used the Greek script, or, more precisely, the Attic-Ionic alphabet, from the fifth century BC onwards. These texts - all of them undeciphered so far - include a fragmentary inscription from Samothrace, the inscription from a ring found at Ezerovo (Fig. 11a), and a grave monument from Kijolmen. Although Greek and Latin became current in Thrace, some Thracian tribes continued to use their mother tongue as late as the sixth century AD.

History of the Thracians

Since the Thracian language has certain Indo-European features, the beginnings of the history of the Thracians are usually associated with the penetration of the Indo-Europeans into the Balkan Peninsula. This probably took place during the Eneolithic and Early Bronze Age, i.e. in the period between the fourth and the beginning of the second millennium BC. There is archaeological evidence of complex cultural and ethnic movements in the eastern and central parts of the Balkan Peninsula in that period, although none of the cultures which emerged at that time can be regarded as the immediate parent of the Thracian culture. Neither did any culture indicating the existence of a large and homogeneous ethnic community develop in the eastern regions of the Balkan Peninsula in the subsequent centuries. The archaeological finds from the Thracian territory dating from the fully-developed

Bronze Age and from the beginning of the Iron Age, between 1600 and 800 BC, are neither particularly numerous nor very specific; they are similar to the finds from the central parts of the Balkan Peninsula and the Danubian region, so that they cannot be reliably associated with the Thracians.

If it is true that *thre-ke-vi /ja* in the Linear B texts means Thrace, it follows that the Greeks were acquainted with the Thracian territories already at the end of the fourth century BC and that the ethnonym Thracians, a general term for the tribes in the eastern parts of the Balkan Peninsula, had already become current. At present there are only a few finds indicating contacts of these tribes with Greece and the eastern Mediterranean. The weapons found in the Thracian territories include rapiers of the same form and workmanship as the rapiers made in Greece between 1500 and 1200 BC. The references to the gold and silver war gear of the Thracian kings in Homer's *Iliad* have not been corroborated by archaeological evidence. Two hoards discovered in the eastern parts of the Balkan Peninsula can be, however, associated with the period immediately after the Trojan War; one of them is the 'treasure' from Vlcitrn (*c.* 1200 BC) and the other is a hoard from Kazicena - Sofia (900 BC).

The Vlčitrn 'treasure', consisting of thirteen ritual gold vessels weighing 12.5 kg, was probably the property of an exceptionally distinguished person, a tribal chief, a king, or a high priest acquainted with the eastern Mediterranean civilization.

The Kazičena hoard is considerably more modest and consists of a copper kettle, a ceramic bowl, and a large gold cup, imported, no doubt, from the east.

Archaeological explorations have shown that the number of hilltop settlements fortified by deep moats and defence walls became increasingly numerous in the mountainous parts of Thrace, and particularly in the Rhodopes, from the middle of the eleventh century BC. Early Iron Age open-air shines with niches and altars among rocks, sometimes decorated with incised figures of men and women, birds, and various symbols, have also been discovered. Some megalithic monuments, chiefly dolmens, in which tribal chiefs and members of their family were probably buried, also date from that time.

The archaeological material found in these settlements and graves is, however, very scant and consists mostly of hand-made pottery decorated with fluting or impressed or incised geometric ornaments. The characteristic pottery with horn lugs, ribs, and impressed decoration, common in the region from the Danube to the north-western regions of Asia Minor testifies to complex ethnic movements in these territories, which classical sources and modern historiographers associate with the Frisians, Moesi, Kimmerians, Treri, and Bithynii. It was only after the Greek colonization of the northern shores of the Aegean, the Propontis, and the western coast land of the Pontus that the population of the eastern parts of the Balkan Peninsula became finally stabilized, and it is only from that time onward that the history of the Thracians can be traced.

From the mid-seventh century BC Greek colonies began to spring up on Thacian shores, usually on the sites of former Thracian villages - Abdera, Maronea, and Aenos on the coast of the Aegean; Perinthos, Selybria, and Byzantion on the Propontis; and Salmydisos, Apollonia, Mesembria, and Odessos on the Pontus (Fig. 9). About 550 BC the Athenians colonized the entire Cherronesus: the regions rich in mineral ores round the mouth of the Strymon were also colonized a little later. In the majority of cases the native Thracian population coexisted peacefully with the colonists and even adopted the Greek culture. From the end of the sixth century the Greeks, and particularly the Athenians, sought to cement their friendly relations with the Thracians by matrimonial ties, too. The further Greek-Thracian rapprochement was, however, suspended by the events associated with the expedition of King Darius I of Persia against Scythia in 513/512 BC.

In order to subjugate the Scythian lands, Darius advanced with a great army from Cherronesus toward the mouth of the Danube, subduing all the Thracian tribes along the way - the Thinoi, the Odrysai, the Skyrmiads, and the Nipsae. The Scyths soon forced Darius to retreat. Pursuing the Persian army, they reached the southern part of Thrace and came to the territory of the Apsinthoi and the Dolonkae. Darius crossed to Asia Minor, but he left a considerable part of the Persian army in Thrace under the command of Megabyzos, who succeeded in making all the maritime towns and adjacent Thracian tribes tributaries to Darius. The Persians built Doriskos, a stronghold in the lower reaches of the Hebros, whence Darius's successor Xerxes launched his expedition against Hellas in 492 BC. Almost all the Thracian tribes joined the Persian forces in this expedition, and the route along which the army advanced came to be regarded by them as an object of veneration. After the defeat of the Persians at Salamis (480 BC) and Potidaea (479 BC), the Persian forces retreated rapidly to Asia Minor, but several strongholds in southern Thrace remained in Persian hands until the Athenians, interested in the mines of gold and silver and the control of the Dardanelles, repossessed the territories round Mount Pangaeus and the Thracian Cherronesus in the latter half of the fifth century.

While Darius's and Xerxes's troops marched in Thrace, the north-eastern parts of the Thracian territory saw the development of processes which led, once the Persian power began to wane, to the emergence of the powerful Odrysian state. The Odrysian King

Tereus (*c*.480-455 BC) united a number of Thracian tribes, organized a strong army, and established economic and political relations with his neighbours. In order to secure the northern frontiers of his state, he gave his daughter in marriage to King Airepeithes of Scythia. His son and successor Sitalkes (455-424 BC) extended his father's realm as far as the Strymon, the Danube, the Aegean, and the Pontus. He also constructed roads, promoted commerce, and made a treaty with the Athenians in order to safeguard the southern frontier of his state. He also mustered an army of 100,000 infantry and 50,000 horsemen, with which he devastated a large part of Macedonia, but when he encountered the Triballi, his forces were routed and he was killed in battle. He was succeeded by his nephew Seuthes I (424-415 BC), who made the Odrysian state the richest country between the Adriatic and the Black Sea.

The increasing wealth and power of the Odrysian state - and its close contacts with its neighbours - the Persians, Scyths, Greeks, and Macedonians - is also illustrated by archaeological finds, particularly those discovered in the large cemetery of the Thracian aristocracy at Duvanli. Gold and silver jewellery from Greek workshops and pectorals and vases fashioned after Persian models begin to appear as grave goods already from the end of the sixth century BC. The large mound Kukova Mogila yielded costly objects from

Greek, Scythian, Macedonian, and local workshops, including a silver amphora, a masterpiece of Persian workmanship (Fig. llb). This find is a manifest proof that local chieftains began to amass riches already in the period of the Persian domination.

The archaeological finds from the second half of the fifth century BC, which is the period of the greatest ascendancy of the Odrysian state, come mostly from Greek workshops. The policy of Sitalkes and Seuthes II, and particularly their alliance with Athens, contributed to the Hellenization of the Thracian royal household and of the entire Thracian culture. Sitalkes had a Greek wife, his son became a citizen of Athens, and the children of eminent Thracians often bore Greek names. On the other hand, the Greeks frequently married Thracian women, and Thracian blood flowed in the veins of some distinguished Athenians, e.g. Thucydides or Themistocles. Ancient myths were supplemented with appropriate episodes emphasizing the close relationship between the Thracian and the legendary Athenian kings. Sophocles represented the fate of the Thracian King Tereus in a new light, and so did Euripides when he dramatized the story of King Rhesus. The close alliance between the Thracians and the Greeks was manifested in the religious sphere as well: the cult of the Thracian goddess Bendis was introduced into the Athenian port of Pireus, and the goddess Kotyto was worshipped in Corinth and Athens.

The Athenian influence on the Thracian court remained strong even during the disintegration of the Odrysian state in the fourth century BC. After the death of Seuthes I, the Odrysian state was divided into three parts, and the kings who reigned in them sought supremacy by attaching themselves either to Athens or to the Macedonian kings. Thus Seuthes II (405-391 BC) compelled the Thynoi to recognize his authority and extended the territory of his state at the expense of his rivals. Kotys I (383-360 BC) succeeded - with the support of the Athenians - in regaining the pristine glory of the Odrysian state. In order to win over the chieftains of independent Thracian tribes and of the neighbouring Triballi and Getae, Kotys gave them great riches. The splendour of Kotys's court, his wealth and diplomatic activity are best illustrated by the costly vessels bearing his name which have been found in the territories not included in his state - in Gorovo, Letnica, Lovech, Vraca, and Rogozen (Fig. 12).

After Kotys's death the Odrysian state disintegrated again: Kotys's son, Kersebleptes, ruled in its north-eastern part, while the military commanders Amadokos and Berisades became kings of its south-eastern and south-western parts respectively. King Philip II of Macedonia took advantage of the discord among the Thracian kings and subjugated the entire Thrace between 352 and 342 BC. In order to consolidate his grip, Philip built the town of Philipopolis in the upper reaches of the Hebros and fortified the town of Kabyle in the Tonzos (modern Tundza) valley. Thrace was organized after the model of Persian satrapies: the Thracians paid taxes and supplied soldiers, and the Macedonian elite retained possession of those places only in which it had special interest. The greater part of the Thracians acquiesced in the new situation and took part in the expedition of Philip's son Alexander the Great against Persia, but some tribes in the highlands sought to regain their independence on several occasions. The dangerous insurrection of the Thracians organized by Scuthus III in 325 BC, the vassal king of Odrysius, was suppressed, after great struggle, only in 313 BC by Lysimachos, one of Alexander the Great's successors, who pacified Thrace after his victory over Seuthes and incorporated it into his realm.

All the towns founded in Thrace during the fourth century BC were modelled on the Greek city-states, and all the official inscriptions in them were written in Greek. These towns became cultural centres from which Greek culture emanated as far as the highland northern and north-western provinces of Thrace. Seuthes III founded *c.* 320 BC the first large Thracian town Seuthepolis, which was modelled after Greek towns. The Thracian aristocracy continued to procure luxury goods from the workshops in Asia Minor and Greece, and demonstrated its wealth and status by the building of monumental tholos tombs, frequently with several chambers and an entrance corridor, in which the deceased were buried with costly jewellery and war gear (Fig. 13). Not far from Seuthepolis, at Kazanlak is a tholos tomb with frescoes modelled on Greek monumental painting, and a man and two women with gold Hellenistic jewellery were buried in a tholos tomb near Mesek. Nine gold vessels, weighing 6.1 kg. and decorated with relief representations of human and animal figures, made by Asia Minor craftsmen from Lampsakos in the Dardanelles, probably for Seuthes III, were discovered at Panagyuirishte.

The high level of the Thracian culture was maintained until the death of Lysimachos in 280 BC. That fatal year marked the beginning of the long agony of the Thacian people and state. Already in 279 BC, the Celts, a powerful West European people that settled in the Danubian region in the course of the fourth century BC, irrupted into Thrace and devastated the Greek towns on its shores. After that they founded the Celtic empire in Thrace with its capital in Tylis. In spite of the frequent insurrections of the natives, they remained the lords of Thrace until 212 BC when they were finally expelled to Asia Minor. The Odrysian state could not be, however, easily restored, for the greatest powers of the time coveted the Thracian territories - first King Philip V of Macedonia, then Antiochus III, lord of the East, and, finally, the Romans. Philip V launched an expedition in 212 BC, seeking to subjugate all the towns in Thrace between the Strymon and Cherronesus, which he succeeded in achieving by 203/202 BC. The Odrysian chiefs were compelled to make an alliance with Philip, but as he was waging a war against the Romans, the Thracians also gained a powerful enemy. In the time of the third Macedonian war with Rome, Perseus, the son of Philip V, made an alliance with the Odrysian king Kotys II. When the Romans gained a victory at Pydna in 168 BC, Kotys made a truce with the victors and recognized their sovereignty.

From that time on the Thracian kings became henchmen of the Romans, whose aim was to annex the entire Balkan Peninsula to the Roman state. It was through the support of the Thracian rulers that the Romans succeeded in subjugating all the free tribes in Thrace and in the Lower Danubian region in the course of the first century BC. As a reward, the Roman state helped them maintain their authority. About 15 BC Thrace got the status of a client state. When the warlike Bessi, led by Dionysos's priest Vologaises, rose, in 11 BC, against their chieftains Rhauskuporis II and Rhiometakles I, the Romans quelled the rebellion in blood and set up Rhoimetalkes I as king. After his death in AD 12 Augustus divided the Thracian state: the rule of the southern part was entrusted to Kotys, and the northern part was given to Rhausuporis III. As a result of their contentions and of the discords among their successors, the Romans abolished the Thracian state in AD 46 and organized Thrace as an imperial province.

The Thracians spent all their energy in the struggle for independence against the Celts, the Macedonians, and the Romans between the third and the first century BC. As a result, the incorporation of Thrace into the Roman Empire took place without any friction or resistance, and the long period of peace which followed improved the economic position of its inhabitants and contributed to the gradual enrichment of their culture.

The Romans founded an exceptionally small number of towns in Thrace (Aprus, Deultum, Augusta Traiana, Hadrianopolis); on the other hand, they constructed good roads, which made possible easy traffic and an extensive diffusion of goods. This led to the rapid Romanization of the native population, which lived mostly in small settlements and villages. The Romanized Thracians adopted all the elements of Roman culture, apart from the funerary rites, for they continued to bury their dead in the traditional way, under large mounds. The population structure gradually changed: the number of foreigners increased in the period between the first and the third century, while the share of the native population dropped drastically because of the slave trade and the recruiting of men, first for auxiliary and then for regular troops.

Greek was still the predominant language; Latin inscriptions were comparatively rare and consisted mainly of dedications to emperors or texts referring to imperial governors.

From the early third century onwards Thrace was constantly exposed to the incursions of the barbarians living of the left bank of the Danube and in the Pontian regions. The Goths, the Carpi, and the Sarmatians devastated Thrace repeatedly between AD 235 and 271. It was only in the time of Diocletian and his successors that peaceful conditions began to prevail. At the beginning of the fourth century Thracia was organized as a *dioecesis* divided into six provinces: Europa, Hoemimontus, Rhodope, Thracia, Moesia II, and Scythia. This *dioecesis* was more extensive and had a larger population than the former province of Thrace, for it included the territories as far as the Danube, which were settled by the Mysi and the Gatae. The strategic importance of Thrace increased after the foundation of Constantinopolis on the Bosphorus in 330. Constantine the Great and his successors built a number of strongholds in it hoping that it would become a powerful bulwark capable of stemming the barbarian forces threatening the Roman empire from the east and the north.

From 364, however, the Goths, the Alani, and the Huns began making incursions into Thrace. Emperor Valens was killed in the crucial battle with the Goths at

Hadrianopolis in 378, and the Roman army was routed. The following year Theodosius I drove the Goths out of the diocese of Thracia, but they savaged it again in 391, 395, and 400. In the first half of the fifth century the Huns, led by Attila, devastated Thrace on several occasions, and in the second half of the same century the Eastern Goths penetrated as far as the province of Rhodope and threatened Constantinople in 483. From 481 onward the diocese of Thracia was repeatedly invaded by Bulgarian forces, first united with the Huns, and later in conjunction with the Slavs and the Avars. Wars against them were waged with changeable success throughout the sixth century. Between 540 and 550 a number of strongholds was constructed in all the six provinces of the diocese of Thracia, but the barbarians succeeded in pulling down their defence walls already in the following decades. Emperor Heraclius succeeded in stemming the Slav and Bulgarian inroads for a time, but after his death the Bulgarians, led by Asparuh, crossed to the right bank of the Danube in great numbers and finally subjugated all Thrace in 679. The Thracians themselves, however, ceased to exist much earlier. They succeeded in preserving their ethnic identity until the fourth century because their traditional religion was still vital; once they abjured their gods and became Christians, they were rapidly assimilated by the barbarian invaders.

The Greeks thought, certainly not without good reason, that the Thracians were particularly gifted for art and that they were an unusually pious people. These features of the Thracians are embodied in Orpheus, the most famous mythic singer, musician, and poet, and also the most ardent devotee of Apollo - the god of light, measure, order, legality, and artistic inspiration - and Dionysos - the god of fertility and eternal rejuvenation of nature, who dies to be reborn and who guarantees immortality to his adherents.

Historical sources tell us that Thracian kings were great patrons of art, and the objects of great artistic value found in the graves of eminent Thracians show that the same can be said of the Thracian aristocracy. The Thracian music must have been, according to myth, both enchanting and very specific. Thracian painting and sculpture, however, was not as highly esteemed. All the art objects dating from the sixth-fifth centuries BC which have been discovered in the Thracian territories were made by Persian, Scythian, Etruscan, or Greek masters. Gold and silver plate, as well as silver jewellery were procured for the rich Thracians mainly from the workshops in Asia Minor or in Greek colonies on the shores of the Aegean, the Propontis, and the Pontus. On the other hand, all the works of monumental architecture and painting in

Thrace were either made by Greek masters or inspired by Greek models.

From the fourth century BC onwards objects fashioned in the so-called animal style became especially popular (Fig. 14). This style, used primarily in the decoration of horse gear and shields, was not, however, limited to Thrace; it was popular in all the territories from the northern shores of the Pontus to the Alpine regions. Although the animal style is not specifically Thracian, archaeological finds show that it was widely adopted in Thracian workshops and that it became in time the most striking feature of Thracian art. Its main themes in the fourth and third centuries BC are fights between animals and birds (lion, bull, snake, eagle) and representations of hunters and horsemen (Fig. 15a). Mythical heroes or deities are shown in an archiving style: the proportions are awkward, the face is frequently in profile with the eyes show *en face*, and perspective is disregarded (Fig. 15b).

The collapse of the Thracian states marked the end of the Thracian art. After the second century they adopted Hellenistic and Roman culture, and their spirit survives only in the monuments associated with religious rites.

In the reconstruction of the Thracian religion we depend on the evidence provided by classical authors, epigraphic monuments, and archaeological finds. The basic structure of the Thracian pantheon, such as it was from the end of the seventh to the middle of the fifth century, was described by Herodotus, who mentions only one god by name (Plistor) and identifies the other Thracian deities with Greek gods (Ares, Dionysos, Artemis, Hermes). It has now been proved that the Thracian Artemis was in fact the goddess Bendis or Kotyto, while the names of the Thracian Ares, Dionysos, and Hermes have not been established.

The Thracian tribes were so disunited that we must assume the existence of numerous local deities and cults, not integrated into a pantheon accepted by all. The Thracians, like all the Indo-Europeans, worshipped the god of heaven and his wife. This supreme god is referred to as Sbelsurd in inscriptions and votive monuments. His wife, identified with the Greek goddess Hero, had a separate cult in Thrace. This is shown by the tradition of her priest Kosingas, who threatened his adherents that he would make a high ladder and climb to heaven to complain to the goddess of their disobedience.

The cult of the Sun existed from very early times, for Homer mentions Apollo as a god of the Thracian Kikones, and later authors refer to a Thracian Helius. A god of light, named Sitalkes, was also revered, and a hymn compiled in his honour has been preserved.

We know best two Thracian deities who were included in the Greek pantheon in the fifth century BC - goddesses Bendis and Kotyto. Thracian women offered to Bendis sacrifices wrapped in wheat straw, and a festivity, consisting of a procession, horse-races with torches, and nocturnal orgies, was celebrated in her honour. The cult of goddess Kotyto was also of an orgiastic character and involved the dressing of men in female clothes.

A vegetation deity, akin to the Greek Dionysos, was particularly revered in Thrace. This god presaged a fertile year by a violent fire, and he also guaranteed eternal life to those initiated in his mysteries. The famous shine of the Thracian Dionysos on Mount Pangaeus was in the possession of the tribe of the Satrai, but its priests belonged to the tribe of the Bessoi. It had a prophetess similar to Pythia at Delphi.

Another well-known shrine of that deity was in the Rhodopes, in the territory of the Thracian tribe of Bessoi. This shrine was visited by Alexander the Great and the father of Emperor August.

The cult of the god Asklepios became particularly popular in the time of the Roman domination. Although Aesklepios is supposed to be of Thracian origin, it is more likely that he replaced some Thracian deity or demon healer named Darron or Derrones. Inscriptions and historical sources provide evidence that the Thracians worshipped river and fountain deities. The best-known river gods were Hebros, Stfymon, and Nestos, who are represented in the genealogies also as progenitors of famous mythic heroes.

The most widespread cult was, however, that of the so-called Thracian Hero. He was worshipped as an almighty god, a healer, saviour, and protector of livestock and vegetation. His real name is unknown. He is most frequently referred to as the Hero, and he is identified with Asklepios, Apollo, Dionysos, or Sylvanus. Since he is closely associated with the mythic king Rhesus, he is supposed to be a personification of the Thracian rulers. A number of the representations of this deity - mostly votive reliefs rating from the period between the fourth century BC and the early decades of the fourth century AD - have been preserved. The greatest number of monuments date from the Roman period. They represent the god as a mounted young man, either hunting or in a resting position. A dog attacking a boar and a tree round which a large serpent is coiled are frequently represented beside the horseman (Fig. 16). The inscriptions accompanying these representations usually refer to the Thracian Hero as *kyrios* (lord), *soter* (saviour), and as *iatros* (healer). He is sometimes also called *megas theos* (great god), as the Thracian chthonic deity Darzalas worshipped in Odessos (modern Varna).

The Thracians believed in the immortality of the soul. They imagined the afterlife as a merry feast in the company of gods. This was probably reflected in their bravery and neglect of life. The weapons and drinking cups found in their graves show that they really believed that they would participate in pitched battles and jovial feasts.

Priesthood had an important role in the religious and political life of the Thracians. Priests were deputies of the gods and counsellors of the rulers. Their power and influence were, however, destroyed at the end of the first century BC. Soon after that, the Thracians, left without their priests and kings, began to identify their deities with Roman gods and goddesses and also included into their pantheon some Oriental deities, primarily Sabazios, Kybele, Dolichenus, and Mithra.

Towards the end of the second century Christianity became established in the major towns. Only the warlike Bessoi, dwelling in the inaccessible highlands of north-western Thrace, held on to their traditional religion for a long time. When the Christian missionaries, after much toil, succeeded in converting them, too, to Christianity, the last glimmers of Thracian spiritual and religious life were extinguished. Only the language of the Bessoi - the *lingua Bessorum* - survived into the sixth century, and its traces are still discernible in the languages of the Balkan people. Neither did the Thracian religion vanish completely with the disappearance of the Thracians: some of its essential elements, particularly those associated with the cult of the Thracian Dionysos and the Thracian Hero - can still be recognized in the customs, oral traditions and Christian legends of the South Slavonic peoples.

The fact that the Thracians deeply impressed their contemporaries, especially the Greeks, and that they have left distinct vestiges in the culture of the present Balkan peoples vows that their historical role was far more important than the scant accounts of classical authors and the available archaeological evidence indicate. The Thracians, like the Illyrians, share the fate of many illiterate peoples whose history is short and inadequately known not because it was unimportant, but because it was written by aliens. Modern scholarship is yet to do justice to the historical role of these two great palaeo-Balkanic peoples.

ILLUSTRATIONS

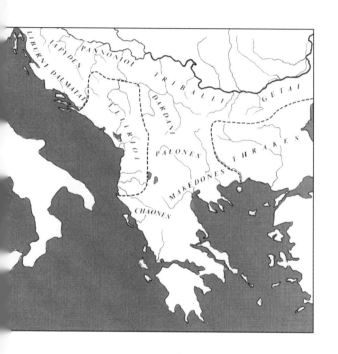

Fig. 1 Palaeo-Balkanic peoples and their territories

1. Byllis   7. Olcinium
2. Apollonia   8. Shkodra
3. Pelion   9. Buthoe
4. Scampis   10. Doclea
5. Epidamnos   11. Rhizon
6. Lissos

Fig. 2 Tribes and towns in Illyria

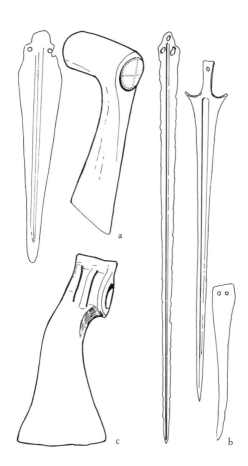

Fig. 3a Electrum bodkin and silver battle-axe from a grave in Mala Gruda (Montenegro)

Fig. 3b Bronze swords from Pazok and Komsi and a curved bronze knife from Dukat in Albania (after Albanien, 29a, 29b, 30)

Fig. 3c Bronze axe of the Shkodra type from Shelcan in Albania (after Albanien, 8)

a

b

c

Fig. 4a Gajtan, a stronghold in Albania (after Gj. Karaiskaj, Monumentet, 14, 1977, pl 2,3)
Fig. 4b Walls of Rhizon (Montenegro)
Fig. 4c Town of Byllis with Hellenistic and Roman defence walls (after A. Base, Monumentet, 11, 1975 pl. 2)

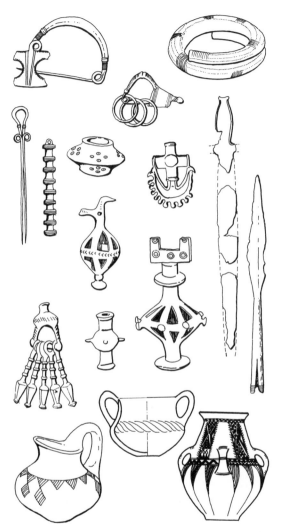

Fig. 5 Weapons, jewellery, and pottery of the Glasinac, Mati, Kukës-Drilon and Kuc-Zi cultures (after Albanien, Abb. 11)

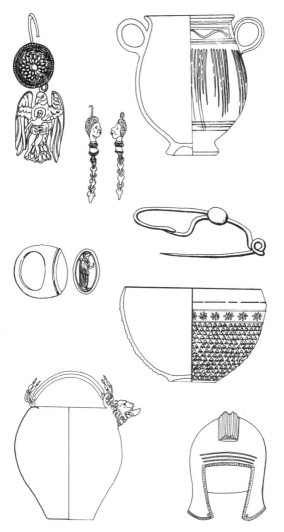

Fig. 6 Weapons and jewellery from the graves at Buthoe and Gostilj (Montenegro)

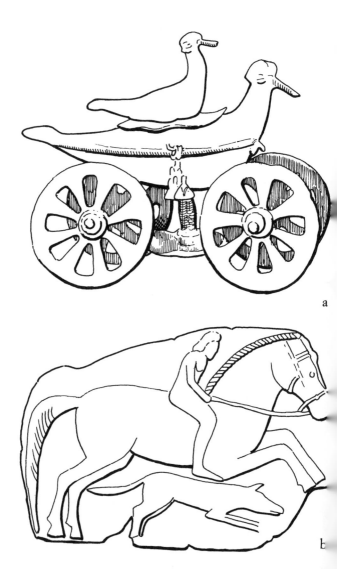

Fig. 7a Bronze chariot from Glasinac (Bosnia)
Fig. 7b Amber pendant from Lisje Polje (Montenegro)

c

d

Fig. 7c Clasps from Gostilj (Montenegro)
Fig. 7d Ring from Momšići (Montenegro)

c

d

Fig. 8 Funeral monuments from Komini (a, b) and
Kolovrat (c, d) in Mont

1. Abdera
2. Maronea
3. Mesambria
4. Ainos
5. Perinthos
6. Byzantion
7. Hadrianopolis
8. Apollonia
9. Deultum
10. Kabyle
11. Augusta Traiana
12. Seuthopolis
13. Philippopolis
14. Odessos

Fig. 9 Tribes and towns in Thrace

Fig. 10a Tattooed Thracian woman, red figure crater, Villa Giulia, Rome

Fig. 10b Thracian soldier, red figure crater, Metropolitan Museum, New York

Fig. 10c Orpheus among the Thracians, red figure crater, Charlottenburg, Berlin

Fig. 11a Gold ring from Ezerovo (Bulgaria) with a
Thracian inscription in Greek letters
Fig. 11b Anfora (gilt) from Divanli (Bulgaria)
Fig. 11c Silver goblet from Bukovci (Bulgaria)

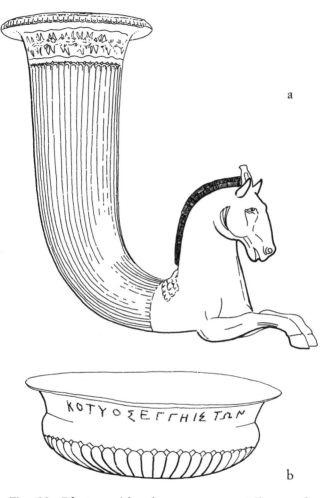

Fig. 12a Rhyton with a horse protome (silver and gilding) from Borovo (Bulgaria)

Fig. 12b Silver vase with the names of King Kotys and master Engeiston written in Greek letters on the neck from Alexandrovo (Bulgaria)

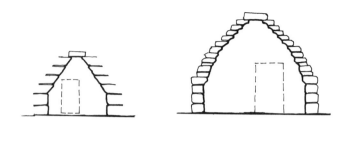

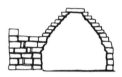

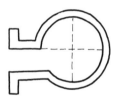

Fig. 13 Tholoid tombs in Thrace (after J. Wiesner, Abb. 17)

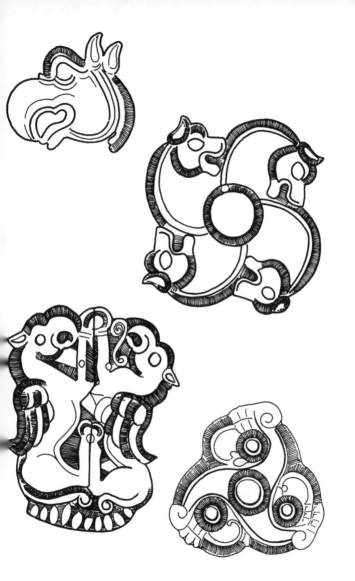

Fig. 14 Ornamental plaques from Letnica, Lukovit, and Bresovo (Bulgaria)

a

b

c

Fig. 15a Ornamental plaque from Lukovit (Bulgaria)
Fig. 15b Ornamental plaque from Letnica (Bulgaria)
Fig. 15c Goddess flanked with animals, a representation
on a silver vase from Rogozen (Bulgaria)

AVR·IOVINVS·MIES
LEG·XI·CLAVDIA·V·P

Fig. 16 Reliefs with the representation of the Thracian
Hero from Glava Panega and Liljače (Bulgaria)

BIBLIOGRAPHY

Illyrians

Albanien, Schätze aus dem Land der Skipetaren. Katalog 1988. Hildesheim.

Cabanes P., *Les Illyriens de Bardylis à Genthios (IVe-IIe siecles avant J.-C.),* Paris 1988.

Ceka H., *Questions de numismatique Illyrienne,* Tirana 1972.

Garašanin, M. (edit.), *Les Illyriens et les Albanais,* Beograd 1988.

Islami, S. *et al., Les Illyriens, aperçu historique,* Tirana 1985.

Krahe, H., *Die Sprache der Illyrier I-II,* Wiesbaden 1955-1964.

Mayer, A., *Die Sprache der alten Illyrier I-II,* Wien 1957-1959.

Pajakowski, W., *Illirowie, Illyrioi, Illyrii proprie dicti,* Poznan 1981.

Papazoglu F., *The Central Balkan Tribes in Pre-Roman Times,* Amsterdam 1978.

Russu, I. I., *Illirii. Istoria, limba si onomastica romanizarea*, Bucarest 1969.

Stipčević A., *Gli Illiri*, Milano 1968.

Thracians

Danov, Ch. M., *Altthrakien*, Berlin-New York 1976.

Detschew, D., *Die thrakischen Sprachreste*, Wien 1957.

Die trakische Silberschatz aus Rogozen Bulgarien. Katalog 1988. Bonn- Mainz-Freiburg-Munchen-Hamburg.

Duridanov, Iv., *Die Sprache der Thraker*, Munchen 1985.

Fol, A., *Demografska i socialna struktura na drevna Trakija prez I hil. pr.n.e.*, Sofia 1970.

Fol, A., *Politika i kultura v drevna Trahja*, Sofia 1990.

Fol, A and I. Marasov, *Thracia and Thracians*, London 1977.

Georgiev, Vl., *The Thracians and their Language*, Sofia 1977.

Gold der Thraher, *Archäologische Schatze aus Bulgarien*. Katalog 1980, Koln-Munchen-Hildesheim.

Hoddinott, R., *The Thracians*, London 1981.

Jumkova, J., *Coins of the ancient Thracians*, BAR Supplementary Series 4, Oxford 1976.

Tomaschek, W., *Die alter Thraker. Eine ethnologische Untersuchung*, Wien 1980.

Velkov, V., *Cities in Thrace and Dacia in Late Antiquity*, Amsterdam 1977.

Velkova, Z., *The Thracian Glosses*, Amsterdam 1986.

Wiesner, J., *Die Thraker*, Stuttgart 1963.

THE SITES

ALBANIA
Institut d'Etudes Historiques de L'academie des
Sciences de L'Albanie - Tirana

BOSNIA AND HERZEGOVINA
Centre For Balkanological Research - Sarajevo

BULGARIA
Thrakologischen Institut Der Bulgarischen Akademie
Der Wissenschaften Und Kunst - Sofia
Archäologisches Institut Der Bulgarischens Akadeie
Der Wissenschaften Und Kunst - Sofia
Academie Bulgare des Sciences - Institut d'Etudes
Balkaniques - Sofia

GREECE

Institute For Balkan Studies - Thessaloniki

Aristoteles University of Thessaloniki, Faculty of
Philosophy - Thessaloniki

ROMANIA

Institut Des Etudes Archeologique - Bucharest

Institut De Tracologe - Bucharest

Academia Romana, Institut Sud-Est Européene -
Bucharest

SERBIA

Albanological Institute - Priština

Balkanological Institute - Belgrade

Archaeological Institute - Belgrade

Centre For Archaeological Research, Faculty of
Philosophy - Belgrade